JANE BODIE

London-born Jane Bodie moved to Australia in 1996. She set up The Other Tongue Theatre Company in Melbourne in 1998 and became the company's artistic director.

Her plays include *FACE2FACE*, *Speaking in Thongs*, *Out Night One*, *Still* (Green Room Award for Outstanding Writing), *Ride*, *Hilt* and *Fourplay*. Her work has been staged worldwide at the Playbox Theatre, Melbourne, Belvoir Street Theatre, Sydney, the Adelaide Festival Centre, the Edinburgh Festival, Theatre Royal Bath and the Dublin Fringe Festival.

Writing for television and radio includes *The Secret Life of Us*, *Crash Burn*, *Out of Sound* and *Seeing Somebody*.

Writing for film includes *Alice* (Dendy Short Film Award) and *Arranged*.

In 2002 Jane became an affiliated writer with the Melbourne Theatre Company and was nominated for both the Malcolm Robertson Award and the Patrick White Award. In 2003 she joined the Sydney Theatre Company, as one of three writers included in their Blueprints Literary Programme.

Jane has now moved back to London. She is working as a tutor on the Royal Court Theatre's Young Writers Programme and with Synergy Theatre Company on their playwriting project in prisons. She is currently on a writer's attachment to the National Theatre Studio.

Other Titles in this Series

Jane Bodie

A SINGLE ACT

NICK HERN BOOKS
London
www.nickhernbooks.co.uk

For Nick Marchand

A Nick Hern Book

A Single Act first published in Great Britain as a paperback
original in 2005 by Nick Hern Books Limited, 14 Larden Road,
London W3 7ST

A Single Act copyright © 2005 Jane Bodie

Jane Bodie has asserted her right to be identified as the author
of this work

Cover image: Nick Warren, N9 design

Typeset by Country Setting, Kingsdown, Kent, CT14 8ES
Printed and bound in Great Britain by Cox and Wyman Ltd,
Reading, Berks

A CIP catalogue record for this book is available from
the British Library

ISBN-13   948 1 85459 884 4 / ISBN-10   1 85459 884 8

A Single Act was first performed at Hampstead Theatre, London, on 16 May 2005 (previews from 12 May), with the following cast:

MICHELLE	Christine Bottomley
SCOTT	Tom Brooke
NEIL	Ian Dunn
CLEA	Rachel Sanders

Director   Anthony Clark
Designer   Patrick Connellan
Lighting Designer   James Farncombe
Sound Designer   John Leonard

Developed with assistance from Sydney Theatre Company's Blueprints Literary Programme

Thanks

My thanks must go to all at the Blueprints Literary Programme, who helped with the initial development of this play, especially Nick and Campion. To Ross Mueller and Julian Meyrick and the original cast in Sydney, who gave so generously at its still unsure and teething stage.

Huge proper humble thanks to Ben and Sally at CB, to Dennis K, and to the director and cast of the Hampstead production – Jo, Lucy, Tony C, Tom, Chrissy, Rach and Ian, whose invaluable and gifted contribution to this final draft made it what it is.

To Nina, Ola, Emily and all those at the Royal Court's YWP, who gave me work and laughed at my jokes. And Rachel and Lucy at the National Theatre Studio.

My eternal thanks must also go to Miranda, Phil, Kate and Thea for late-night pool, love and unerring friendship.

And of course my mum, and Sam, Dad, Annie, D and G for everything else.

And thank you to Frances S. Especially Frances.   J.B.

Characters

SCOTT, *a man in his late twenties*

MICHELLE, *a woman in her late twenties*

CLEA, *a woman in her mid-thirties*

NEIL, *a man in his mid- to late thirties*

Sometime in the near future.

The entire stage area should act as both homes. Either the bedroom or lounge/kitchen area for both couples.

A door stage left should function as a door to a bathroom and on stage right, a door to the outside world.

The rooms should be relatively sparse, symbolic of the kinds of living spaces they are, as opposed to naturalistic.

Though the positioning of each piece of furniture in each room should be similar, the different mood and feel of each home environment should be clearly defined.

Slashes (/) denote the point of interruption, and the dialogue which interrupts it.

Scene One

January.

SCOTT *and* MICHELLE *are sitting in their lounge, as far apart from each other as possible.*

MICHELLE *has a large angry bruise on her face, from the cheekbone to the mouth. The bruise is relatively new and fresh.*

An empty animal cage sits in front of them on the floor.

It should be positioned at an exact middle point between them, its door open.

SCOTT *stares at the cage, unflinching.*

Particular attention should be paid to beats in this scene, so that the sense of heaviness is almost unbearable.

A silence.

A single car can be heard passing.

We hear a car door slam.

SCOTT. Why?

    Pause.

    Why d'ya do it?

    Pause.

MICHELLE. Dunno.

    Beat.

SCOTT. What for?

MICHELLE. I dunno.

    Beat.

SCOTT. To hurt me?

MICHELLE. Maybe.

Beat.

Something like that, yeah.

Beat.

SCOTT. Michelle.

She looks at him, as if waiting for him to speak.

But he's not looking at her.

Michelle, Michelle, Michelle, Michelle, / Michelle.

MICHELLE. / Because this has to stop.

Pause.

Another car can be heard passing.

SCOTT. Looks wrong, with nothing in it.

MICHELLE. Scott. If there's something you want to say to me.

SCOTT. Don't want to look at it.

MICHELLE. I'm here, now.

I'm listening.

He takes his eyes off the cage.

/ Scott?

SCOTT *raises his voice.*

SCOTT. / I DUNNO WHAT YOU WANT ME TO SAY!

Startled, MICHELLE shifts back in her chair.

When she speaks, her voice begins as a whisper and then gradually reaches normal volume.

MICHELLE. I'm going now.

SCOTT. Don't . . .

MICHELLE. I'm not staying, Scott.

SCOTT (*covering his face, with his hands*). Please, Chel . . . don't.

Pause.

MICHELLE. My tooth.

She touches her face.

If I touch it, it'll just, fall out.

She winces and closes her eyes for a moment, then opens them. SCOTT turns his focus back to the rabbit cage.

Isn't there anything you want to say to me?

SCOTT. I love you.

Beat.

MICHELLE. Before I go.

SCOTT. I love you, Chel.

Beat.

MICHELLE. Scott . . . Scott, / please.

SCOTT. / Look I just fucking hit you, alright! I just did.

Now shut your fucking mouth or I'll hit you again!

Blackout.

Scene Two

January, twelve months earlier.

CLEA is standing at the window, as if staring out. But her eyes are focused somewhere on the floor.

She is still wet, from the snow outside.

Occasionally she glances at the TV, which is on, but the sound is off.

The door opens. NEIL stands there in the doorway, with a large camera bag. CLEA looks up.

NEIL. Fuck.

Beat.

Fuck!

Beat.

You're here. You're . . . safe.

Beat.

I tried . . . calling.

CLEA. Me too. I tried / . . . calling . . . too.

    NEIL *reaches into his bag, pulls out his mobile.*

NEIL. / Must have been at least fifty times, and . . . nothing, no signal. / Nothing.

CLEA. / No. Me neither.

    She holds up her mobile, which she has been clutching in her hand.

No . . . signal . . .

NEIL. But you're here, you . . .

CLEA. Nothing.

NEIL. You made it back.

    Beat.

You're . . .

CLEA. Got home about an hour ago. The traffic . . . the street, / everything . . .

NEIL. / I know.

CLEA. I walked. No idea for how long, I just . . . walked.

    Beat.

Lost one of my shoes. My new ones.

NEIL. Did you?

    Doesn't . . . / matter.

CLEA. / But just one. I mean, now neither one of them will be any good, any use, to anyone.

    Beat.

And then . . . you weren't / here . . .

NEIL. It's alright.

CLEA. You weren't here.

Beat.

NEIL. Fuck, what am I doing!

He puts his phone in his bag, drops it on the floor. He comes towards her.

Standing close, he takes her hands.

Hello.

She touches his face, almost tentative.

CLEA (*almost a whisper*). Hello.

He holds her close.

NEIL. You're . . . warm.

CLEA. Am I?

NEIL. I can feel your heart beat.

CLEA. Yes, I think I can feel that.

NEIL. I thought . . .

CLEA. Yeah.

Beat.

Yes.

Beat.

Well, I didn't really, have time to, / to . . . think.

NEIL. / But when you didn't pick up, when I couldn't get a, a . . . I imagined all . . . / kinds . . .

CLEA. / Always thought I'd be perfect in a situation like that, the perfect sort of person to have around.

NEIL. I'm sure you were.

CLEA. No, I wasn't.

Beat.

I just . . . sat there.

NEIL. What else / could you . . . ?

CLEA. / But people were talking. Standing around, talking, to each other.

And then it started to snow.

I didn't even wind the windows down. I left them closed.

NEIL. You . . . you were in the car?

CLEA. I feel like there's broken glass on me.

NEIL. Shit . . . / did you . . .

CLEA. / No . . . I wasn't . . .

Beat.

It's like that, that thing . . . when you, you walk through a spider's web.

And you can still . . . feel it on you afterwards.

Beat.

But I wasn't near enough.

NEIL. Come here. Sit down.

CLEA. I was driving away from it, in a cab.

He leads her towards the couch, still holding on to her.

And I kept the windows closed.

NEIL. Here, take your shoes off. I'll rub your feet.

CLEA. My *shoe.*

Beat.

They sit on the couch. He puts his arm around her, pulls her to him.

NEIL. Come here then, *hop-a-long.*

CLEA. Shouldn't have taken a cab. I wasn't strictly working.

NEIL. On a secret mission, were you?

She looks at him.

What?

CLEA. It's a secret.

Beat.

I'm sorry.

NEIL. What for?

CLEA. Well, it will have to wait now.

I mean, you won't get it till, till after your birthday. I'm so sorry.

NEIL. Clea . . .

CLEA. I'm alright. I'm . . . just a little shaken, that's all.

NEIL. We both are. Bound to be.

Beat.

And probably a little stirred.

CLEA (*laughing quietly*). Yeah.

Beat.

Lucky though.

He looks at her.

Happy birthday.

NEIL. I love you.

She smiles.

CLEA. Knew I shouldn't have worn them. It's the strap on them. It's ornamental, there for the *look* of it. Doesn't actually function, keep the things on, at all.

He is looking at her.

I saw the sky.

Smoke, where the clouds had been, just a . . . moment before.

Beat.

And then you get out.

NEIL. It's alright.

He squeezes her.

CLEA. Thank you, for coming home.

NEIL. I'm sorry that you got here first.

CLEA. And you know I couldn't remember if we said we'd eat in tonight.

She leans her head on his shoulder. They sit in silence.

We could try that new place, with the, the leaflets.

NEIL. That's if they're open.

They both stare ahead in silence.

Fuck.

Beat.

Fucking . . . *Christ.*

He holds her closer.

That . . . that image of you, with just one shoe on, walking through the streets, in the snow.

She looks at him.

CLEA. What?

NEIL. You look beautiful.

CLEA. I hope the driver was alright.

Beat.

NEIL. What . . . what do you mean?

She laughs out loud suddenly, then puts her hand over her mouth.

Clea . . .

CLEA. There we were, me and him. Both of us watching it . . . unfold.

He's looking through the window, at the sky. And then he just gets out, without warning. He gets out, leaves the engine, the meter running and he walks towards, towards where it's happening. He leaves me there.

Beat.

And so I got out and I walked away.

She gets up and goes into the kitchen area. He watches her.

Not sure what I'm going to tell work when they get the cab charge.

She looks back at him.

What they gonna do, take me to court?

NEIL. Just tell them that you were worried, for your own safety.

CLEA *opens the fridge, stares into it, stops.*

CLEA. But I wasn't.

He looks up at her.

I wasn't worried.

And then as I was coming up to the door of the flat, I had this image, of the cab, left there. Like something out of a . . . a *Mad Max* film. This image of it there, engine still running, and . . . crawling . . . with humans, like creatures. Until the body of the thing, was this writhing . . . mass. And they were pulling it apart, for . . . fuel, machinery, salvaging every bit of its carcass, to take back to their kingdom under the ground.

Beat.

And that cheered me up.

Beat.

NEIL. Wow.

CLEA. I think we both need a drink.

Red?

Beat.

Or did you want a white?

She peers closely into the fridge.

Shit.

He looks back at her.

Didn't you put a bottle in here last night?

Beat.

NEIL. I don't . . . / remember.

CLEA. / No, it's alright. It was hiding at the back, behind the cheese.

She pulls out the bottle of white wine.

There's a couple of steaks in here, we could have.

She grabs a corkscrew. She holds it up.

See, for all we know, somebody could have made this out of some recycled bit, salvaged, from a good old London taxi.

She looks at him.

We could have an early night.

NEIL. It wasn't smoke.

She looks back at him.

In the sky. It was a dust cloud, it rose up from the, from the building. It looked like smoke / but . . .

CLEA. / Shit . . . Neil.

NEIL. I was at the office. The view from the window up there was . . . it was like a big-screen TV. But with no other channel.

People had come out onto their roofs. They were leaning over the edge of their rooftop gardens to see whether they should go down, go down to get a better look.

And the cameras were going so fast, all around me, that all I could hear was this one long continual sound, like a, a hum.

And everybody was *on.*

By then the roads were being blocked, bit by bit. You couldn't get close. Because they were trying to clear away the bodies, as fast as they could.

Beat.

CLEA. Fuck, Neil.

Beat.

Fuck. To be there . . . like *that*, to . . . catch / it, like that.

NEIL *shakes his head.*

NEIL. / I didn't . . . I just wanted to see you . . . just –

She approaches him.

CLEA. We're home, Neil. We're safe, and home.

She kisses him on the forehead.

Doesn't bear thinking about.

Beat.

You're sweating.

Beat.

NEIL. Am I?

He runs his fingers through his hair.

Think I could do with a glass of water.

He pushes her gently aside, stumbles to the sink.

He turns the tap on, lets it run with his hand under it.

CLEA. Anyway, you think I'd let anything get in the way of our 7 p.m. Semillon?

Beat.

They'd have to do better than that.

He looks up at her, smiles.

They'd have to kill me first.

NEIL *is staring at the sink.*

That was a bit off.

Sorry. Don't know why I said that.

Beat.

NEIL *suddenly and violently vomits into the sink. He lets his head hang there for a moment.*

NEIL (*weakly*). God . . . sorry.

The lights fade.

Scene Three

December, one month earlier than Scene One.

MICHELLE *is talking on the phone, hushed, so that we can hardly hear her.*

She now has a fallen look, defeated, as if constantly nervous and about to be startled. When she walks, she moves as if the act of walking itself is painful.

As she talks on the phone, SCOTT *lets himself in. She glances back and then goes back to the call.*

SCOTT *is carrying a large box.*

MICHELLE (*on phone and trying to end call*). Yep . . . yep, no problem, that's fine . . . thanks. Thanks.

She puts down the phone.

Beat.

SCOTT. Hey.

Beat.

MICHELLE. Hey.

SCOTT. Who was that?

MICHELLE. Wrong number.

Beat.

Somebody after one of the people that used to live here, I think.

Beat.

Wasn't for us.

SCOTT. Right.

MICHELLE. How was work?

SCOTT. Alright.

Beat.

Na, it was good . . . busy. Glad it's over though. Van gets cold by the end of the day. Lonely.

Beat.

I like that dress.

MICHELLE. Do ya?

SCOTT. I like it on you.

He comes in and puts the box down on the coffee table.

Don't reckon it would look so good on me. Haven't got the waist for it, my shoulders would poke out.

Beat.

So . . . ?

She looks at him, nervous.

Come on. Aren't you going to ask?

Beat.

MICHELLE. What?

SCOTT. Oh . . . *come on.*

MICHELLE. What . . . what do you . . . / ask what?

SCOTT. / The box. *Hello.* Don't you want to know what's in it?

Come on, you'd be dying to know. You know what you're like.

Beat.

So, go on then.

MICHELLE. What is it?

Beat.

SCOTT. What's what?

Beat.

MICHELLE. *Scott* . . .

SCOTT. No.

> *Beat.*

> Come on.

MICHELLE. Alright. Scott. What's in the box?

> *Beat.*

SCOTT. You'll have to open it, open it up and see.

> *Beat.*

> Go on. *Open* it.

> *She looks genuinely afraid.*

MICHELLE. I don't want to.

SCOTT. Why not?

MICHELLE. I hate surprises.

SCOTT. No you don't.

> *Beat.*

MICHELLE. You open it.

SCOTT. God, I lug the thing halfway across town, up the stairs . . . it's a gift, for fuck's sake. I bought it for you. I want you to open it. In front of me.

> *Beat.*

> *She begins to walk towards the box.*

> Won't bite.

> *She stops.*

> (*Laughing.*) No, go on, I'm only kidding. I'm just kidding with ya. Go on.

> *Beat.*

> Want to see your face.

> *She looks at him, unsure.*

> *Then she begins to open the box tentatively, as if it may go off at any second.*

Something moves deep inside the box. She catches her
breath, startled, jumps back. SCOTT *laughs.*

Jesus . . . come here.

SCOTT *goes to the box, as she stands aside. He puts his*
hands inside and pulls out a cage with a white rabbit inside.
The rabbit is obviously startled. It jumps about in its cage.

Happy Easter.

MICHELLE. Shit!

SCOTT. You frightened the poor little thing.

MICHELLE. It's a . . . a / rabbit.

SCOTT. / It'll probably shit in the cage now.

MICHELLE. You bought us a rabbit.

SCOTT. No, I bought you a rabbit.

Beat.

I don't want a rabbit.

Oh look at him . . . he's cute though, those floppy ears. And
hungry, he'd be hungry. He'd want something to eat.

Beat.

What do they eat, anyway . . . rabbits?

MICHELLE. I don't / know.

SCOTT. / They eat carrots, don't they?

Beat.

MICHELLE. Don't know.

SCOTT. Took me ages to find a place that sold them, and then
most places didn't have white ones. And I knew you'd want
a white one. Just knew. You like him, don't you?

MICHELLE. He looks scared . . . maybe you should take him
out.

SCOTT. Thought we could put him outside on the balcony
there. Let him run about occasionally, when we can keep an
eye on him.

Beat.

Should've seen your face.

MICHELLE. He looks scared, Scott.

SCOTT *looks at the rabbit.*

SCOTT. Yeah, well, that's because he's trying to work out what kind of rabbits we are. You like him though, don't you?

He goes to the fridge, gets himself a beer.

Thought we could call him Stu. You know . . . our rabbit, *Stu.*

He laughs.

Be eating out of your hand, any day now.

She has approached the cage. She attempts to stroke the rabbit through the bars. But seems afraid.

I'm parking on this street, this morning, on the way to my first job, and I see this kid getting out of his dad's car, with this box, all excited, can hardly carry the thing.

They take it inside, and I can see him, through the window, open it up. Then he's playing with it, with this, this rabbit. Dad's watching.

And the thing's tame. Like it knows this kid's his . . . master, ears prick up, when he calls his name and everything. Kid's laughing, tickling him, under his tummy . . . laughing.

Beat.

And that's when I remembered. You said you wanted a rabbit.

Beat.

MICHELLE. When I was a kid.

SCOTT. More than anything in the world, you said.

MICHELLE. When I was a kid, Scott.

Beat.

When I was a little girl I wanted a rabbit.

SCOTT. A white one.

MICHELLE. Yeah . . . yeah, and my brother wanted a, a monkey –

SCOTT. A proper Easter bunny.

MICHELLE. Scott . . . It's December, it's almost Christmas.

Beat.

/ Scott.

SCOTT. / Well, there you go, you said you wanted one and I got you one.

MICHELLE. I didn't mean . . . when I was ten. I wanted one . . . when I was . . . / ten.

SCOTT. / And it wasn't cheap.

Beat.

MICHELLE. It's just . . . I'm not sure, where we're gonna . . . whether we should give it . . . water, or . . . something.

SCOTT. Got to admit he's pretty cute though, look at his little nose.

MICHELLE. Maybe we should put him outside.

SCOTT. He likes / you.

MICHELLE. / Ow, shit, shit, he bit me.

SCOTT. Oh . . . come / on.

MICHELLE. / He bit me, with his teeth.

SCOTT. He just . . . licked you. Gave you a kiss.

MICHELLE *examines her finger, puts it in her mouth.*

You'll get that thing. That myxomatosis.

Beat.

MICHELLE. I'll put him outside for the night. Decide what to do with him in the morning.

MICHELLE *carries the cage to the back door, puts it out.*

SCOTT *swigs at his beer.*

MICHELLE comes back into the room. She stands for a moment, just looking at him.

I might have a bath.

Pause.

SCOTT. You're welcome.

Beat.

MICHELLE. What?

Pause.

SCOTT. No really. You're welcome.

Beat.

MICHELLE. It was a sweet thought.

SCOTT. Not what you wanted though.

SCOTT turns away from her, his back to her. She looks at the bathroom door, but doesn't move.

Who did they say they wanted to speak to?

Beat.

MICHELLE. . . . What?

SCOTT. On the phone, before.

Who did they say they wanted to speak to?

Beat.

MICHELLE. I can't remember.

Beat.

He asked if . . . whoever he was . . . after, was here.

SCOTT. And you told him that they were no longer at this address.

MICHELLE. . . . Yeah.

SCOTT. So it was his mistake.

She nods.

So why did you thank him, at the end of the call?

Beat.

MICHELLE. Habit . . . you know, just being . . . polite.

SCOTT. Should get onto the estate agent about that. Make sure they've got a record of the number changing hands. For future reference. Could get annoying, that, if it keeps happening.

MICHELLE (*quietly*). Yeah.

SCOTT. If it keeps happening.

Beat.

Really fucking annoying.

Beat.

MICHELLE *starts to cry, to whimper silently. She doesn't move.*

I'll ring them tomorrow. Sort it.

Beat.

You should have a bath.

Beat.

Should put your bath on.

She looks at the bathroom door, then back at him. She doesn't move.

The lights fade.

Scene Four

February, one month later than Scene Two.

CLEA *and* NEIL*'s bedroom.*

CLEA *is sitting up in bed, with the blankets half-covering her, her knees bent. She is wearing a vest. Her hands and arms are covered by the blankets.*

As some movement starts under them, it appears as if she is masturbating. She has her eyes closed.

Eventually we see a shape of another body under the blankets.

NEIL *emerges from the blankets.*

CLEA *opens her eyes, a sense of her being interrupted.*

CLEA. What?

   Beat.

   NEIL *runs his fingers through his hair.*

   I didn't give a signal or anything. I didn't mean to.

NEIL. No, no it wasn't . . . wasn't anything . . .

CLEA. What?

   He suddenly gets up out of the bed and disappears into the bathroom. He appears in the bathroom doorway with some dental floss.

NEIL. I didn't floss my teeth.

   He pulls out a line of floss.

CLEA. Well, I couldn't tell.

   Beat.

NEIL. But I hate that, that *feeling*.

   Beat.

CLEA. Neil . . . really, I couldn't . . .

NEIL. And you know . . . I think I want a *cigarette*.

CLEA. You don't . . . don't smoke.

NEIL. No. But I want one. *Really* want one.

   Beat.

CLEA. Well, it's customary to have one afterwards.

   He looks at her.

   He goes back into the bathroom.

   We hear the tap running.

   She leans back in the bed.

   It's the crow's feet, isn't it?

Beat.

Unsightly lines, the woman called them. Shone this special light on them, with a magnifying lens. And there they are, magnified. A line, for every case I've lost.

She touches her face.

And anyway, it worked.

NEIL (*still in bathroom*). What did?

CLEA. Because at the end, I bought the cream she was brandishing . . . waving, in front of my starving, malnourished eyes. Bought two jars of the stuff.

He emerges out of the door, flossing his teeth.

Something French, made in Milton Keynes.

NEIL. You look alright to me.

CLEA. / Thanks.

NEIL. / Why the hell would I want a cigarette, after all these years?

CLEA. No / idea.

NEIL. / Haven't wanted one, thought about one, for . . . years.

Beat.

But I just feel like, you know, feel like lighting one up.

CLEA. Well, / you can't.

NEIL. / *Breathing* one in.

CLEA. You can't because we haven't got any.

NEIL. Didn't we used to keep some spare, for guests?

CLEA. That was tampons.

NEIL. / Was it?

CLEA. / And that was in the old flat.

He disappears back into the bathroom.

She shifts in the bed, closes her legs.

He comes back to the doorway, looks at her.

Long day. You're tired probably.

She moves aside to make a space for him in the bed.

NEIL. I feel more awake than I've felt for ages.

He goes back into the bathroom, we hear the sound of a tap running and then he emerges. He comes and sits on the side of the bed.

Sorry about that anyway.

CLEA. I'll keep.

He laughs, quietly.

NEIL. Oh, and I said yes, to Nathan.

She rubs her fingers through his hair.

To helping him out, down at the warehouse.

Nathe said they've got this huge bunch of clothes, that that's what people have donated, over the last few weeks.

CLEA. Well, I'm sure they need someone like you down there.

NEIL. Like me?

CLEA. Place like that, that kind of . . . set-up. All those well-meaning middle-aged women. They'd be crying out for a bit of testosterone.

NEIL. But he said it's electrical goods that people want right now.

Beat.

It sounded mad, on the phone, this . . . rabble, in the background.

Anyway, it'd be good to help, to do something.

CLEA. My little helper.

She kisses his back.

Though I'm surprised you can afford to take the time off.

He gets up, begins to walk round to his side of the bed.

I mean, right now, what with everything, *everything*, still taking twice as long.

NEIL. I said I could do it at the weekend.

CLEA *suddenly looks up at him.*

That I'd give him a hand this weekend.

Beat.

CLEA. Thought we were going to try and get away this / weekend.

NEIL. / Clea, it's Nathan.

CLEA. To the sea.

Beat.

NEIL. And he can't do it on his own.

CLEA. You said that you'd take me away from all this.

Beat.

And anyway, he's not on his own. What about the, the rabble?

NEIL. I want to help. Do something.

CLEA. Of course. Yes. We all . . .

NEIL. I feel . . . helpless, useless, as it is!

Beat.

CLEA. Neil . . .

You're not useless.

Beat.

You're never . . .

He pulls back the blankets, suddenly.

He climbs into the bed beside her.

NEIL. Well, I've said I'll do it now. I can't go back on my word.

CLEA. That's my side.

NEIL *climbs over her, she under him, as if automatically.*

NEIL. Not that I feel like sleeping.

Pause.

CLEA. Maybe I could come and help too.

Beat.

It might pay to have a lawyer on hand down there.

I mean, you know what volunteers are like.

They're all out for themselves.

He smiles, but looks away.

We can go another weekend.

Beat.

When things have . . .

NEIL. And I'm not sure how much use I am to work at the moment.

Beat.

CLEA. What do you mean?

Beat.

You're a good photographer, Neil. Nothing's going to change that.

She reaches out to touch his face.

He flinches.

It's just your Saturn Return.

NEIL. Think I'm too old / for that.

CLEA. / It affects all of us, at some stage. The tell-tale sign, at work, is when somebody starts bringing in their own special tea. Because caffeine, has become the enemy.

Beat.

It's made worse by a vitamin-B deficiency.

Or is that a lack of sexual appetite?

She looks at him.

I won't keep for ever.

I'm organic. Which means that though I taste better, my shelf life is limited. Because I'm preservative-free.

She kisses him on the shoulder.

NEIL. You sure we haven't got any cigarettes?

CLEA. Yes.

Beat.

NEIL. Think I could almost have a tampon right now.

She smiles.

Their heads come together to kiss.

She puts an arm around him.

Shit!

NEIL *suddenly pulls away.*

Shit. Your . . . nails, one of your . . . nails, it pricked me.

She withdraws, slightly.

Sorry, I'm a bit tense.

CLEA. Come here. I'll give you a rub.

NEIL. I think it might hurt, to . . . to laugh.

CLEA. No jokes, I promise.

He shuffles over, so that he is sitting with his back to her, in between her legs. She begins to massage his shoulders.

Think you've pulled something. *Over-*flossing.

He starts to laugh, despite himself.

NEIL. / . . . Ow.

CLEA. / Don't be a baby.

He begins to relax. Slowly the massage begins to get more sensual.

He opens his eyes.

NEIL. Nathan said they're going to give each volunteer a different section of clothing to sort out. They're doing it by name, so for example, *Nathan*, he'll be Nathan, on Nylons.

CLEA. What about you?

NEIL. I put my hand up for Neil on Knitwear.

CLEA. I think Neil on Knickers has more of a ring to it.

He stares ahead.

NEIL. Can't stop thinking about it. What he said. About people wanting electrical goods.

CLEA *continues massaging.*

But when it went off, you see, it wasn't just the building itself that got damaged.

CLEA *stops for a second.*

Because right next door, underground, there's this . . . sub-station. This thing that controls all the power, electricity, to the surrounding areas. That must have been part of the plan, because during something of that size, thousands of volts were fed into people's homes, into . . . well, whatever they had plugged in . . . on.

CLEA. Kind of . . . brilliant . . . when you think / about it.

NEIL. / But imagine it. *Imagine*, that you're . . . making a piece of toast, ironing, listening to a CD . . . typing something on your computer, at that moment when it happens.

He looks at her.

CLEA. I'm imagining.

NEIL. Whatever it is that you're doing, would be tainted . . . would *feel* tainted.

And every time you wanted to use that thing, it would be like . . . like having to plug into it. Like having to go back, back through it all over again.

Beat.

CLEA. He lost a son.

Beat.

NEIL. What?

CLEA. Roberto . . . he's one of the . . . he delivers sandwiches, sandwiches and . . . fruit, to the office. Comes round with a little basket every day. Always cheerful. Of course he charges a bit extra, for bringing it *to* us, for enabling us to avoid the, the lunchtime rush.

And anyway, he doesn't turn up last week. And we're all waiting, starting to get a bit . . . hungry. And of course none of us thought, I mean, it's been almost a month.

And because it's not like at the beginning. When you couldn't complain if some . . . file, came in late, or a client wasn't giving you the answer, the paperwork you needed. I mean, back then, you even gave the couriers the benefit of the doubt, because you know . . . they could have, they could have lost someone.

Beat.

And it turns out he did. His son, Mario. He has this great accent when he says his name. Anyway, he'd been in hospital this whole time, burns. Lung damage. Nobody in the office knew. And Roberto, and his family, they'd been waiting for him to pull through and anyway, it turns out he didn't.

But then he's back in yesterday. He's suddenly there at my desk with my favourite, turkey on rye. And he tells me, smiling, that the best way to deal with it, with the loss, is to get on with your normal everyday life.

And that's why he's back at work.

NEIL. Christ.

CLEA. Makes you think.

NEIL. Yeah.

CLEA. And shouldn't you . . . your . . . *bunch* be doing a story on people like *that*. Fathers . . . that are going on, despite what's happened to their lives, their families. Something positive and . . . uplifting, you know, to give to people, in the midst of all this . . . doom.

NEIL. Is that what you think people need?

CLEA. It's what they want.

Beat.

I bought two sandwiches off him, and an apple.

She kisses the side of his face.

NEIL. You hate apples.

CLEA. I know.

He closes his eyes. She continues massaging, but softly.

I could go by myself, couldn't I? I could drive down there and just . . . wing it. Find some old B&B to stay in, turn off the mobile and stare at the sea.

I'd like to see the sea.

Beat.

Neil . . . ?

NEIL *is asleep, his head fallen to one side.*

CLEA *brings her head round to his face, to confirm that he is out. Then she kisses him lightly on the cheek. She stays sitting there, cradling him in her arms.*

And maybe I'll just stay here, with you.

She holds him there.

The lights fade.

Scene Five

July, five months earlier than Scene Three.

The bedroom is in semi-darkness. We hear a rustle as SCOTT *enters the room.*

MICHELLE *suddenly rolls over in the bed and turns the bedside light on.* SCOTT *is standing there, at the end of the bed, jeans and a thin vest on. For a second she looks afraid, and then witnessing* SCOTT's *docile state, she breathes.*

MICHELLE. Shit.

Beat.

Scott, you scared me.

Beat.

What you doing?

SCOTT. Sorry.

Beat.

MICHELLE. Sweetheart, what are you doing?

SCOTT. Dunno.

MICHELLE. You've been . . . where have you . . . where've you been?

SCOTT. Dunno.

MICHELLE. I didn't hear you get up . . . I didn't . . .

SCOTT. Couldn't sleep.

MICHELLE. Didn't even realise you'd gone.

Beat.

SCOTT. I couldn't sleep.

MICHELLE. Was I snoring again?

SCOTT. Na.

Beat.

You weren't.

MICHELLE. Come here.

SCOTT *doesn't move. He stays standing at the end of the bed.*

You shouldn't do that, just get up in the . . . you're not even properly dressed.

SCOTT. Fucking mad out there . . . fucking hot . . . people everywhere, not doing anything.

MICHELLE. Scott . . . it's the middle of the night.

SCOTT. I came round this corner, and this bloke kind of comes at me, doesn't say nothing, just looks at me, stares, like he's waiting. Like he's waiting for me to say something. And then he says, 'It's alright. I understand. I . . . understand.'

And then he walks off.

Lucky for him too, because I was about to . . . jumpin' out at me like that in the middle of the night. I felt like shouting after him, shouting . . . 'Yeah, mate, it is alright. Well, I'm alright. But to be honest I'm not so sure about you.'

Beat.

'I'm alright.' Don't know what he thinks he was fucking doing.

MICHELLE. Come here. Come here, Scott. You're . . . you're sweating.

SCOTT. You pushed me away.

MICHELLE. / What?

SCOTT. / You rolled away from me.

MICHELLE. Scott, I was asleep.

SCOTT. Just wanted to talk to you.

Beat.

You look nice when you're asleep.

MICHELLE. What, when I'm . . . snoring?

SCOTT. Sometimes look at you and think . . . what did I do to deserve her?

How did that happen?

Beat.

MICHELLE. Sweetheart, get into bed.

SCOTT. How did that happen?

Beat.

MICHELLE. Scott . . .

SCOTT. And you're right. You should go back to your job, if you want, if you really want to. It's alright that you, that you miss it, miss the kids and that. I just thought . . . but you're right to want to have something, something other than . . .

MICHELLE. Sweetheart –

SCOTT. You should stand your ground, good that you do that.

MICHELLE. Sometimes . . . sometimes it's not so easy.

SCOTT. It's just me, just me, what I'm like. It's not you, not your . . .

MICHELLE. I know. I know.

SCOTT. I'd never hurt you. I wouldn't.

Beat.

Couldn't stand that, wouldn't fucking forgive myself. I'd die.

You're the best thing that's ever happened to me.

Don't know how you stand it.

Beat.

MICHELLE. Come here, I'll warm your side up.

She moves to the other side of the bed.

Get into bed. Keep me company.

He sits on the side of the bed, facing her.

SCOTT. I'll protect you, you know.

Beat.

MICHELLE. From what?

SCOTT. From all of it. I'd never let anything . . . I mean, I'd die first.

She laughs quietly.

What?

MICHELLE. Nothing.

SCOTT. What? I would.

MICHELLE. I / know.

SCOTT. / I'm being serious.

MICHELLE. That's twice you said you'd die for me . . . not
    that I don't appreciate it / but . . .

SCOTT. / I mean it, Chel, I would.

Beat.

MICHELLE. How many lives you got?

SCOTT. Don't ever leave me.

Beat.

MICHELLE. Scott . . .

SCOTT. I mean it.

Beat.

MICHELLE. You're the one that's sneaking out in the middle
    of the night.

SCOTT. I wanted to get you something, wanted to get
    something, for you, so that it'd be here, when you woke up.

Beat.

Couldn't find anything.

MICHELLE. It's the night, Scott, everything's / closed.

SCOTT. / Yeah, well, I realise that now, don't I!

Beat.

MICHELLE. I get you. I get to wake up to you every morning.

She reaches out and touches his face.

I get that.

*He leans into her, like a child. She cradles his head in her
arms.*

SCOTT. You'd tell me, wouldn't you, if I wasn't what you
    wanted . . . you'd tell me . . . to my face?

She strokes his head, almost lullaby-like.

MICHELLE. All those people out there . . . out there now.

Looking for . . . trying to, protect . . . whatever's left.

Find some, some reason for being left behind.

SCOTT. I found you.

MICHELLE. You did.

Beat.

Now get into bed, Scott. I have to be up early, tomorrow.

SCOTT. Do ya?

Beat.

What for?

MICHELLE. That thing, I told you.

Beat.

SCOTT. What?

MICHELLE. It's just a . . . like a, a check-up thing.

SCOTT. What, at the doctors'?

MICHELLE. Yeah.

Beat.

SCOTT. Did you tell me?

Beat.

MICHELLE. I didn't want to worry you.

Beat.

Just one of those routine things.

Beat.

SCOTT. So, it's nothing to worry about?

Beat.

MICHELLE. No.

SCOTT. I'll drive you.

MICHELLE. No, it's alright.

SCOTT. No, I'll drive you.

MICHELLE. It's just a check-up, Scott, that's all. Be boring.

Beat.

I'll go on my own. Be easier.

She leans forward and rubs her nose on his, an Eskimo kiss.

Be easier.

SCOTT. You're the best thing that's ever happened to me.

Beat.

Dead straight.

She kisses him on the mouth. When she pulls away he is crying, silently.

MICHELLE. Shhh now.

She wipes his face. Then kisses him again.

SCOTT. How come you always taste like that?

She strokes his hair.

The lights fade.

Scene Six

March, one month later than Scene Four.

CLEA *enters through the front door of the apartment. She stands there, the light from the hall outside, shining into the room.*

We can just make out NEIL, *sitting in the couch in the dark.*

CLEA. You're here.

Beat.

You've got the light off.

NEIL. Have I?

CLEA. Neil, you know you've got the light off.

He lights up a cigarette. CLEA *comes into the room.*

Where did you go?

NEIL. For a walk.

She turns on the light. NEIL *flinches slightly.*

Was one of those walks, when you don't really *go*
anywhere. It's about leaving somewhere. About being
somewhere else.

Beat.

And then at some point you find you're home.

CLEA. You're smoking.

NEIL *looks around the room.*

NEIL. Shit. That's where the smoke's coming / from.

CLEA. / You bought a whole packet of cigarettes.

NEIL. They don't sell them individually any more.

Beat.

CLEA. How many have you smoked?

NEIL. Twelve.

He looks at the one he is smoking.

Thirteen.

Beat.

Lucky, for some.

CLEA *goes to the fridge. Pulls out an open bottle of wine,
grabs two glasses and begins to pour the wine.*

CLEA. Well, the music didn't improve. And somebody brought
out some of those mini quiches, that are always still half-
frozen. You have to eat around the outside and put them
back. So that by the end of the night there are these bits of
half-nibbled quiche everywhere, discarded, at random.

Beat.

Quiche hearts, all alone and unwanted.

She begins undoing her hair.

NEIL. Was there music?

CLEA *stops pouring the wine.*

I didn't notice.

CLEA. I think Rachel was hoping that you'd just wandered off for a bit, that you were coming back. I told her you might. I was hoping you would.

NEIL. I'm sorry.

CLEA. I knew you wouldn't.

CLEA *approaches the couch, with two glasses of wine.*

Well anyway, they liked the present. Rachel said that wrapping it in newspaper was very . . . very –

NEIL. Japanese?

CLEA. *Environmentally sound.* And Adam did that thing he does, you know that . . . thing, when he opened the present. '*Bowls,*' he said, 'Clea and Neil have bought us *bowls.*'

She holds up a glass for him.

NEIL. *Boules.*

They're called *boules.*

She is still holding the wine.

It's a different word, different game altogether.

CLEA. See. You should have been there.

She motions to the wine.

I'm no good at these things on my own.

She puts the wine in front of his face.

NEIL. No. Thank you.

She holds the wine glass there, for a while. Then brings her arm down.

CLEA. So I told Adam that he should count himself lucky that we hadn't bought them a goat.

NEIL *looks up.*

I told them that next year they should prepare themselves for a goat . . . or a children's bicycle, that we might even make them part-owners in a . . . well . . . or something like that, for a village in need.

NEIL. Were they amused?

CLEA. What's wrong?

NEIL. I'm tired.

CLEA. I think they really did like the present.

NEIL. Good. I'm glad.

CLEA. *Boules.*

He looks at her.

Why were you sitting in the dark?

NEIL. If you think about it, turning the light on, actually involves more of a decision than leaving it off.

Beat.

CLEA. I missed you.

NEIL. I wouldn't have danced, whatever they played.

CLEA. You never dance. I still missed you.

CLEA *sits on the edge of the couch.*

NEIL. Always liked watching you dance in that dress.

He puts a hand on her back.

CLEA. I tried the margaritas and you were right, they weren't properly frozen. And far too much salt.

She pulls a face, as if eating something bitter.

That's my *too-much-salt* face, pretty good I think.

NEIL. It's bordering dangerously close to your *too-much-ice-cream* face.

He smiles. She touches his face.

CLEA. I brought you some cake.

She gets up and goes to her bag, takes a small parcel out. She holds it up. He says nothing. She goes to the fridge and places it in there.

Your going-home present.

Beat.

You eaten?

NEIL. I'm not hungry.

She closes the fridge door.

CLEA. Maybe I was ready to leave too.

NEIL. You were dancing.

CLEA. I was making an effort.

NEIL. Well. I couldn't.

Beat.

I'm sorry.

Beat.

I watched those people / tonight.

CLEA. / Those *people* are our friends.

NEIL. Well, I watched those friends. Sat and . . . watched
them.

At one point Andrew came over, and he sat down at my
feet, just sat there in silence. And I thought – there, at least
you, Andrew, have a, a soul, somewhere deep inside you. At
least you and I are sharing this moment, even if you can't
express it in words and I was touched by that. I really was.

And then he looked up at me and he raised his glass and
you know what he said?

'So Neil, how come you're always in the right place at the
right time? When you gonna let some other cunt get a shot
of the action?'

Beat.

CLEA. Was that when you left?

NEIL. No, I waited for Sonia to squeeze my arse and tell me
that she still wanted to fuck me.

CLEA. Well, she does still want to fuck you. At least she was
being honest.

NEIL *closes his eyes,* CLEA *strokes his face.*

I still want to fuck you. Life and soul of the party. Or not.

CLEA *joins him on the couch, places her legs over his.*

They're having a baby, Neil. Rachel and Adam are going to have a baby.

I think that's something to celebrate.

NEIL. Do you?

CLEA. Yes.

Beat.

For God's sake it happened two months ago.

NEIL *gets up off the couch and goes to the fridge and pours himself a mineral water.*

Nobody's particular nice when they're drunk, my darling. Not when you're sober. That's why I plan to never give up drinking.

Beat.

Did you know that Evian, *Evian,* spelt backwards is *naïve*? I wonder if they meant that?

NEIL. It wasn't because they were drunk.

He comes back to the couch, sits down, but away from her.

CLEA. I thought it might do us good, to get out.

She moves closer, attempts to snuggle into his neck, he doesn't respond.

And I'm sure the cause will survive without us, for a night.

NEIL. It's not a cause, it's not about it being a . . . / cause.

CLEA. / No but come on, you have to admit that you're . . .

NEIL. What . . .

Beat.

That I'm what?

CLEA. Well, it's like living with fucking Sting.

No reaction. She stops, sits back.

Sometimes people don't want to talk about things. And that's their way of dealing with it, that's their . . . statement.

NEIL. *That* says nothing.

CLEA. Well, it's obviously managed to piss you off.

She laughs to herself.

But you know, we should have bought Adam the goat. Just to see his face when he opened the card.

NEIL *gets up again.*

Come on, it would have been funny.

He turns to her, suddenly.

NEIL. There were people there, Clea, just before.

Beat.

And then they weren't. They weren't there.

Gone.

Beat.

And I feel that we have to deal with that now, with what that means.

I do, at least.

Beat.

CLEA. Okay.

Beat.

I'm sorry . . . I didn't . . .

NEIL. No.

Beat.

CLEA. *Hey . . .*

He looks at her, waiting for something.

Let's go to bed.

He stays looking.

She unzips her dress.

NEIL. I'm going to stay up for a while.

Beat.

Watch the news.

Beat.

CLEA. / Neil . . .

He sits down in front of the TV.

NEIL. / Just for a bit.

She looks at him, and then turns and exits into the bedroom.

CLEA (*calls out*). It won't tell you anything you don't already know.

CLEA *continues talking from the bedroom, but* NEIL *is not looking.*

I can still taste that margarita, on me. I'm ready salted.

NEIL *stares, fixated by the news on the screen.*

CLEA *appears in the bedroom doorway, naked.*

She stands there, her skin glowing in the light of the TV. But he doesn't turn round.

He grabs the remote control from the coffee table.

He begins to turn the sound up. She watches, waits.

It will just go on, you know. Whatever we do.

Beat.

NEIL (*distracted by the screen*). Hmm?

CLEA. And anyway, half of the world doesn't even know it's happened.

He points the remote at the TV screen.

He turns the TV over to another channel, but much of the same and then turns the volume up, still without looking back.

The lights fade, except for the light of the TV screen.

Scene Seven

April, three months earlier than Scene Five.

SCOTT comes into the lounge/kitchen first, he seems angry, riled.

He leaves the door open and paces the room.

Eventually, MICHELLE follows him in. She is carrying two bags of shopping and she seems frightened, shaken. She puts down the bags as if trying not to make a noise.

SCOTT. You fucking happy now!

Beat.

Well, are you?

She begins unpacking the shopping.

Don't you fucking ignore me!

Beat.

I'll do that!

She stops unpacking the shopping. She stands with her back to him.

(*Quieter.*) I'll do it.

Beat.

Gonna get the silent treatment now, aren't I?

Beat.

Aren't I!

MICHELLE. I don't know what you want me to say.

SCOTT. Yeah, that'd be fucking right, the silent treatment all the way home, then the fucking . . . helpless number. That'd be right. Lay it on thick, make me feel bad, go on, make me beg.

MICHELLE. I'm not –

SCOTT. Like a dog, that has to beg.

MICHELLE. I'm not . . . not trying to . . . make you . . . *feel* anything, / I'm not . . .

SCOTT. / What does that mean?

MICHELLE. I'm . . . just . . .

SCOTT. What?

MICHELLE. I didn't . . . mean to . . . to . . . I just wanted . . .

SCOTT. Chel, you're talking shit, you're not making any sense.

MICHELLE (*almost crying*). Scott, I'm . . .

SCOTT. What?

MICHELLE. Why are you . . .

SCOTT. WHAT?

Beat.

MICHELLE. I don't know what I did.

SCOTT. That's right, you got no idea.

MICHELLE. I . . . don't.

SCOTT. SPEAK UP. I can't hear you. It's hardly an equal conversation, is it, if one of us isn't making any sense?

Beat.

I mean, why fucking ask me, why fucking ask me in the first place, if you're not even interested in my opinion?

Beat.

MICHELLE. I wasn't thinking.

SCOTT. Oh, don't give me that.

MICHELLE. I wasn't. I'm tired . . . I'm sorry . . . sorry if you had a bad day.

SCOTT. My day was fine. Thanks. Perfect.

Beat.

MICHELLE. I'm tired, Scott. I'm tired.

SCOTT. Got to have things just the way you want them. Don't want to change . . . compromise. I mean, isn't that why I came? So we could share that stuff, together, as a fucking couple!

Beat.

But no, gotta have it your way.

Beat.

MICHELLE. You're right.

SCOTT. You'll be saying it was me, made you give up your job next. That it was my idea.

Beat.

MICHELLE. You're right. I was being selfish. I was thinking of myself.

Beat.

I'm sorry.

Pause.

SCOTT. Well, you got your fucking pasta, and that's the main thing.

Beat.

So let's just drop it now, let's just leave it. It's finished.

Beat.

MICHELLE. It isn't.

SCOTT. It fucking is.

Pause.

She puts her hand up to her nose, holds it. She looks at him and then begins to walk towards the bathroom door. He stands, blocking her path.

MICHELLE. I want to wash my face.

SCOTT. Looks alright to me.

MICHELLE. Scott, I've got a . . . my . . . my nose is bleeding . . .

Beat.

I'm bleeding. Please.

Beat.

SCOTT. I'll get you something.

He doesn't move.

Beat.

Why? Why is it bleeding?

MICHELLE. Why do you think?

Beat.

SCOTT. Shit.

Beat.

I'll get you something. You sit down. I'll get it.

MICHELLE. Scott, I need to go to the toilet . . . I need to . . .
I'm, / I'm . . .

SCOTT. / Should put something cold on it. You . . . you sit
down. I'll get something.

Beat.

*He begins to walk slowly to the kitchen bench. She seizes
the opportunity and makes a run for the bathroom and
slams the door.*

SCOTT *looks at the door for a moment.*

Chel?

Beat.

Chel?

Beat.

CHEL!

We hear the tap go on, in the bathroom. SCOTT *goes to the
door, and he waits for a while. When he speaks he lowers
his voice.*

Chel, come on . . . let me look at it. If it really is bleeding,
if you . . . you should let me look at it, and I can . . . I can
go and get you something.

Beat.

If you want.

Beat.

Come on. Come on, Chel, I'm sorry, okay.

Beat.

I'm sorry.

We hear the toilet flush.

He looks at the door. The tap starts running again.

Chel . . . ?

MICHELLE (*from the bathroom*). GET AWAY FROM ME!

He strokes the door, with a finger. And waits.

He starts to bang on it with his fists.

SCOTT. Chel, Chel, let me in! Please.

His voice begins to raise and break.

Let me FUCKING IN!

He leans his face on the door, breathing deep, almost in tears.

(*Quieter, almost a whimper.*) Let me in.

The lights fade.

Scene Eight

April, one month later than Scene Six, same month as Scene Seven.

CLEA *is sitting on the couch. She's drinking a glass of wine and staring ahead.*

NEIL *is standing at the window, looking out, as if at something.*

Music plays quietly in the background.

NEIL *glances out once more. He then slowly comes over to the couch.*

He sits down, beside her.

He begins to leaf through a newspaper, slightly avidly and shaking his head.

NEIL. Well, it's done now.

Beat.

Not that it's finished.

Beat.

Just wish they could have, at least, looked into ways of minimising some of the pollution, before, before . . . pulling it, tearing the whole thing down.

But then these people only see the immediate result of their actions. They can't see that what they're doing now is only going to cause further damage, long term.

The phone rings.

NEIL *looks at it, slightly agitated.* CLEA *sees him do this.*

It suddenly stops.

NEIL *acknowledges this and then goes back to his paper.*

There is a pause.

CLEA. I went to the supermarket.

NEIL. And now apparently asthma's on the rise, all around the central area, where they've done it, allergies in general. And that's not going to go away. And people are angry . . . they're angry about the way things are being dealt with. And they have a point.

CLEA. Their vegetables and fruit look quite good these days.

NEIL. They don't know who to trust.

CLEA. They're obviously trying to win us back. I mean, I don't normally look at them, now that we get the delivery.

Beat.

NEIL. But then, they've achieved what they wanted.

Nobody has to look at it any more.

Beat.

CLEA. I didn't get anything. At the supermarket.

NEIL *looks up from his paper*.

They've got these displays everywhere, Easter displays. Eggs, for every occasion.

Beat.

I'm in the Italian section, spaghetti . . . sauces, that kind of thing, and there's this woman beside me. She's standing so close to me, it's as if she doesn't notice I'm there. And she looks . . . paper thin, as if she's *barely* standing. And then I realise, it's that she doesn't realise *she's* there, it's not *me*. This woman actually isn't aware that she has a . . . a presence.

Beat.

Then she picks out some pasta, the spiral kind, and she turns. And there's this man, watching her, at the end of the aisle. She holds up the pasta to him, and he shakes his head. Shakes it, to the pasta, and he turns away. And she holds on to it for a moment. And then she's just about to put it back on the shelf, but instead she checks, she checks if he's still watching, and he isn't. And then, she puts it in her trolley.

And I think, *good on you*. If you want it, that pasta, you have it, put it in your trolley, you . . . *go* for it.

NEIL *is watching her by now, really watching*.

But then he comes back.

And of course, I want to know if he's going to notice, the pasta, see that she's put it in. And he does. He looks down into the trolley and he says something to her, but I don't catch it, because I've moved away by now, so that I can watch . . . un-noticed.

And then he says something again, but louder, quite loud, like a bark. And she says something back, but in a sort of whisper and she doesn't meet his eye. And then she begins to lean into the trolley, reach into it. And I think, no . . . no, hang on a minute, don't give up . . . don't give in, now that you've decided to make that choice, that single act of defiance . . . don't take it back. You mustn't. You mustn't.

And then he hits her.

I mean, he really hits her. And we don't know it's coming . . . me, or her.

But he gets it, bang on, like he actually hooks her with his fist, catches her face in its . . . in its arc. And I hear it, his fist, hit the side of her face. Hear the thud of the impact and it's not like you think it's going to sound. Not anything like it.

And she, she almost goes down . . . she staggers a bit. And he steps towards her and tries to put his arms out, to . . . to hold her up, I suppose. He wants to hold her now. I can see that.

But she doesn't let him. She manages, somehow to straighten herself up. And she walks away from the trolley, walks to the end of the aisle and disappears. And he doesn't even watch her go. He just stares down at the shopping.

Beat.

And I realised then, that I'd seen her before, just before in the pharmacy section. She looked different then.

She was browsing, looking at stuff, as you do. But then she picked up this, this thing, held it in her hand. I noticed that you see, because we both picked up one of the things, and read the instructions on the back, at the same time. We both picked up a pregnancy test.

NEIL *is still looking at her. She takes a large swig of her wine.*

NEIL. Clea . . .

She looks at him.

Was she . . . was she alright?

CLEA. I don't know.

Beat.

Got half the way home in the car before I realised I was crying.

And then you weren't here.

NEIL. I was just, just out.

Beat.

Went out for a / walk.

CLEA. / You weren't here!

NEIL. I'm sorry.

CLEA. And then my period started, so that must have been it.

Why I was crying.

He reaches out a hand to her. She drinks from her glass.

Apparently women have far too many periods these days, as it is. Traditionally, you see, at my age, I'd have been pregnant . . . six or . . . seven times, by now, at least.

And that's not counting miscarriages . . . abortions.

And then we start our periods earlier and we menopause later . . . so all in all, we're having far too many of the things, in the one lifetime.

So a couple of days late . . . well, it's a reprieve.

Beat.

NEIL. I wish you'd told me.

CLEA. I'm telling you now.

Beat.

And it sorted itself out.

NEIL *reaches out and touches her face.*

She puts her hand over his hand. A moment.

NEIL. They're building one of those fountains, in town.

She begins to guide his hand down her neck and towards her chest.

Those fountains they build up against walls to look . . . like rain. This wall of rain always *falling* . . . but going nowhere, it doesn't have an end point, it just keeps going, round and round. It doesn't stop.

NEIL *looks down at his paper and then back up, she lets go of his hand and it falls away from her.*

Once more he puts a hand up to her face, she places her hand over it.

Anyway, now's hardly the time to be bringing a child into the world.

Beat.

She begins moving his hand, as if it is stroking her face, though mechanically.

Slowly she begins to hit herself in the face, with his hand, each hit getting increasingly harder, until the impact has some force and begins to make a sound.

(*Under his breath.*) Clea . . .

She is now managing to hit herself with some considerable force.

(*Almost a whisper.*) Clea.

Eventually NEIL *manages to pull his hand away.*

He looks down again, at his hands.

I'm sorry.

And then back at her.

CLEA. No you're not.

He turns away from her.

The lights snap to black.

Scene Nine

March, one month earlier than Scene Seven.

SCOTT *is bringing in a box from the hall.* MICHELLE *is putting crockery from a box away in the kitchen. We see that the lounge is full of boxes.*

He puts down the box. She keeps filling the cupboards.

MICHELLE. I said I'd help with those last ones.

SCOTT. I'm just happy you know where things are supposed to go.

MICHELLE. It's kind of obvious.

SCOTT. Wouldn't have a clue.

MICHELLE. Cups, you see . . .

She holds up a cup.

They go here, on the . . . cup rack.

She places them in the cupboard.

Right next to the plates.

She motions to the pile of plates in the cupboard.

SCOTT. Yeah, you might just need to go through it a couple of times.

He smiles at her.

MICHELLE. Anyway, I like it, finding a home for things. Finding where they fit.

Beat.

You can hear the birds out here. Hear them . . . *chirping*. It's nice.

SCOTT. *You're* nice. Standing there, filling my cupboards . . . with *your* things.

She stops, turns to him.

MICHELLE. You . . .

You need a shower.

Just, you're a bit . . .

SCOTT. What?

She starts to smile.

MICHELLE. Just a bit.

He smells his armpits.

SCOTT. I thought you women liked that.

He comes towards her. She grins.

MICHELLE. I'm not complaining.

He wraps his arms around her.

I'm just saying that you could do with a shower.

He holds her tighter.

I wasn't complaining.

He kisses her.

Weird out there. That . . . wind.

SCOTT. S'gonna rain.

MICHELLE. Is it?

SCOTT. Yeah. Wind first, then the rain. Always like that in March.

Still, it usually turns out my busiest month, what with all the marquees and stuff. It's when people start gearing up to get married, you see, preparing. They think it's gonna have cleared up for their special day, come June.

Think the world's gonna stop.

But you know what they say.

Beat.

'As it rains in March . . . so it rains in June.'

And it's true.

Think people would've worked it out by now, would do the sensible thing, and go for another month.

You watch, it'll bucket it down any minute.

MICHELLE looks behind him.

MICHELLE. I didn't think I had so much stuff. Didn't look like that much.

He looks back at her stuff.

SCOTT. I got you something else.

He goes to his bag, gets out an A to Z – brand spanking new.

He takes it over and presents it to her. She laughs.

So that you can always find your way home.

MICHELLE. Thanks.

She opens the book and takes a piece of paper from the first page.

What's this?

Beat.

SCOTT. Nothing much.

MICHELLE (*grinning*). What is it?

Beat.

SCOTT. Well, you said you'd never had your name on a, a lease, a . . . place.

She looks at the piece of paper.

No big deal, it's just a yearly thing, nothing . . . I just thought you'd like it.

MICHELLE. I do, I just didn't . . . I / do.

SCOTT. / You don't have to. Just thought it'd be a nice . . . you know, if I made it . . . official. You can change your mind.

She play-cuffs him round the face. He reacts, mock hurt.

MICHELLE. Now that wouldn't be a very good start would it, not when I've just moved in?

He grins. She flicks through the A to Z.

I should have a look at all the buses and stuff though, trains. Took me almost an hour and a half to get into work yesterday. And I can't always rely on you to drive me.

SCOTT. I don't mind. Anyway, you don't have to go in if you don't want.

Beat.

I mean, you don't have to go into work, if. You know, if you want more time, to yourself. We don't need the money.

MICHELLE. I like my job.

SCOTT. I know, but I mean, you could have more time off, to do the things you –

MICHELLE. I want to keep doing what I'm doing, doing . . . my job. I'm good at it.

I like it, Scott. That's why I do it.

SCOTT. I know . . . I just mean . . . you know, what you said about being part-time and that. I'm just saying.

She looks at him.

Beat.

MICHELLE. Well . . . anyway, for the moment I just need to work out a better way of getting in there . . . from all the way out here.

SCOTT. It's hardly the outskirts. And at least we've got grass, trees, we can see the fucking things.

MICHELLE. No, I don't mind –

SCOTT. They're gonna knock it down, you know, next few weeks.

Beat.

Right there in the centre of things. Just pull the whole thing down.

Obviously feel it's been up there long enough, the . . . the powers that be.

Should have done it when it happened, I reckon, got it over with. Though fuck knows how they're gonna do it, right in the middle there, with everything all around it.

Probably be worse than the fucking blast itself, when the thing finally comes down, you know, down to earth.

Beat.

She is watching him now.

MICHELLE. / Yeah.

SCOTT. / Bang!

She is slightly startled.

Wouldn't catch me at it, anyway.

MICHELLE *resumes putting stuff in the cupboards.*

He gets a beer out of the fridge.

All that . . . inner-city living.

She takes the beer from him, takes a swig.

Sorry, do you want one, for yourself?

MICHELLE. No, it's alright, I'll just share yours.

SCOTT. . . . *Ours.*

She takes a large swig, grins.

Steady on there, though.

She opens the fridge, looks at it.

MICHELLE. What were you thinking of having for dinner?

SCOTT. Hadn't really thought about it. Thought maybe we could go out.

She closes the fridge.

You know, celebrate, our first official night together.

MICHELLE. I'm going out tonight.

Beat.

With Fiona and Kath. I told you that. Told you last week.

SCOTT. No. No, I don't –

MICHELLE. Well, I did, I did tell you, Scott.

SCOTT. Well, I obviously forgot, didn't I?

Beat.

MICHELLE. You know I see them once a week.

SCOTT. Yeah, alright, but . . . / tonight?

MICHELLE. / It's our girls' night, you know that. Was the only night Fiona could get a babysitter. We organised it last week. I did check with you. I did, / Scott.

SCOTT. / Yeah, ALRIGHT!

She steps back, startled.

Beat.

MICHELLE. Sorry . . . I just . . .

He grabs another beer from the fridge, yanks the top off. She stands perfectly still.

SCOTT. I mean, that's just perfect. Our first night together in our new home.

He goes into the lounge area.

I'll just get a takeaway then. Hang out with your boxes, until you decide to come home. When you're ready.

MICHELLE. I'm sorry. It's just that it's –

SCOTT. Yeah. Your girls' night.

He goes into the bathroom and closes the door with some force.

She looks at the door for a moment, shaken. She breathes.

She looks to the front door, then back at her pile of boxes.

She puts a hand over her mouth, stifles a sound.

Then she walks towards the pile of boxes of her stuff.

She takes out a book, holds it to her chest, so that we see that she is breathing fast and hard. She looks at all her stuff.

We hear a chain flush. She quickly puts the book back in the top of the box and heads back to the kitchen bench.

The bathroom door opens.

SCOTT *stands in the doorway and watches her for a moment.*

SCOTT (*quietly*). I'm a fucking idiot, aren't I?

Pause.

It has started to rain outside, quietly. MICHELLE *still doesn't look at him.*

Told you it was gonna rain.

Beat.

Just wanted to spend the evening with you, make it special, you know? Our first night and everything.

We can do it another night, yeah?

Beat.

MICHELLE (*quietly*). Yeah.

SCOTT. We got loads to choose from now, eh?

Pause.

Didn't mean to upset you.

MICHELLE. No.

Beat.

It's the rain.

Makes me sad.

He laughs, quietly.

SCOTT. Silly bugger.

She laughs, gently.

MICHELLE. Yeah.

Beat.

SCOTT. Sun'll come out in a minute.

He smiles at her.

Then it'll piss down all over again.

Beat.

Why would anyone want to get married in June, you reckon?

She looks up at him, standing in the doorway.

The lights fade.

Scene Ten

December, eight months later than Scene Eight, same month as Scene Three.

The physical positioning of NEIL *and* CLEA *from* CLEA's *entrance in this scene should mirror or echo, in as much as possible, their movements in Scene Two – as if they are replaying the moment at which* NEIL *returned home on that day, though with each of them playing the other's role by assuming the other's physical position.*

NEIL *is standing, holding the phone, as if a call has just ended.*

He replaces the phone in its cradle, and goes to the window.

He stands there for a while, peering out, as if at something.

CLEA *comes in from work. She closes the door and stands there in the doorway.*

She looks exhausted and slightly damp.

NEIL *stays looking out the window.*

CLEA. Fuck.

Long beat.

Fuck!

He turns to her.

You're here. You're home.

Beat.

I wasn't sure if you'd . . . if you were out . . . in it.

Beat.

I tried calling.

NEIL. Me too. I tried . . . calling . . . too.

She reaches into her bag, pulls out her mobile.

Your phone was . . . off.

CLEA. It's snowing, out there.

NEIL. It said to try later.

CLEA. I mean it's really snowing.

Beat.

I think it's going to settle.

Beat.

But you're here, you . . .

NEIL. I got home about an hour ago.

Beat.

The traffic . . . the . . . street . . .

Beat.

/ Everything.

CLEA. / Everything.

They look at each other. A moment.

CLEA *comes in out of the doorway.*

I know.

Beat.

And then I remembered we said we were going to have dinner together tonight. That you said . . .

So I left. I just left the office.

She hangs her coat up, puts her bag on the couch.

NEIL. It's alright.

She takes off her shoes.

What they going to do, take you to court?

Beat.

CLEA. That's another pair of shoes gone.

He looks back out the window.

Anyway, I'm sorry.

NEIL. Hey, I'm not complaining.

He looks back at her.

I wasn't complaining.

Beat.

Thank you for coming home.

Beat.

CLEA. Sorry that you got here first.

Beat.

She goes into the bedroom.

NEIL *stares back out the window, for a while.*

She emerges, with a vest on and climbing into some tracksuit trousers.

She stands in the doorway.

He looks back at her.

NEIL. Long day though?

CLEA. Something like that, yeah.

NEIL. It's over now.

She comes over to the window, stands beside him.

CLEA. What's going on out there?

He turns to her.

NEIL. I'm just . . . I was just keeping an eye out.

CLEA. What for?

NEIL. I was missing you.

He smiles. She looks out the window.

CLEA. It's settling.

She goes to the fridge, opens it and stands there, staring into it.

NEIL *looks back.*

NEIL. What you after?

CLEA. Not . . . sure.

NEIL *comes over to her. He reaches into the fridge, past her.*

NEIL. There.

She watches, as he takes out a bottle of wine.

Or did you want a red?

Beat.

CLEA. White's fine.

She goes and sits on the couch.

He begins to open the wine.

NEIL. Not long now.

Beat.

Three weeks from now and we'll be out of here.

Our own private hideaway, down by the sea.

CLEA *stares ahead.*

Our own . . . view of it. For five days. Five whole days and nothing, nothing to bother us, nothing to worry about.

CLEA. I don't know about that.

He looks at her.

I mean, there's preparation. There's . . . packing, shopping.

There's spare bedding to think about.

He pours the wine.

NEIL. You hungry? I bought us some supplies, on the way home.

Beat.

CLEA. *Supplies?*

NEIL. Just got us a few things.

Beat.

CLEA. Good to be prepared, for all possible outcomes.

He comes over, holds out a glass of wine for her.

NEIL. Bought us a couple of steaks.

Long beat.

So, how hungry are you?

She ignores the wine.

CLEA. Sorry, I'm a bit . . . I've been feeling a bit . . . off, all day.

Beat.

Not sure why.

NEIL. You need to eat.

Beat.

I did miss you.

He puts the wine down on the table, sits beside her.

I do miss you.

Beat.

And I'm sorry that work's been getting to you.

He strokes her shoulders.

CLEA. Been getting to all of us.

Then her arms.

He closes his eyes.

We're all having to deal with it.

She closes her eyes.

NEIL. I can feel your heart beat.

CLEA. Yes . . . I think I can feel that.

He opens his eyes.

NEIL. We could have an early night.

She opens her eyes.

Beat.

You're . . . shivering.

Beat.

CLEA. Am I?

NEIL. You should put something on.

Beat.

I'll get it.

He gets up, goes into the bedroom.

She leans forward and fiddles with his camera bag that is sitting on the table.

He comes back with a jumper, hands it to her.

CLEA. You left this behind this morning.

NEIL. Was thinking we'll have to get some proper holiday snaps.

She looks at him.

He reaches forward and takes the camera bag off the table.

CLEA. Yeah.

He takes the camera bag into the bedroom. Then re-emerges.

He sits on the edge of the couch.

NEIL. We could spend the first few days of the new year down there, by sleeping. We could do that, couldn't we, if we wanted?

Beat.

Just . . . sleep. We used to be good at it.

CLEA. It's one of the most common things that people experience.

Beat.

After an event like this.

He looks at her.

Sleeplessness.

Perfectly understandable.

NEIL. But why should anyone blame us for getting on with things?

She gets up and goes to the window.

She lights up a cigarette.

Thought you were stopping.

She looks back at him.

CLEA. I haven't really started.

NEIL. Could make that the last one you smoke.

She blows the smoke in his direction.

CLEA. Then what'll I do for my New Year's Resolution?

Beat.

NEIL. I could cook those steaks up now.

CLEA. Won't they take a while?

NEIL. They're minute steaks.

Beat.

Should only take a minute.

He grins. He goes to the kitchen, takes the steaks out of the fridge and gets out a pan. She turns and looks out the window.

We got a phone call earlier . . . one of the . . . tenants, from the flat . . . wanting to know about getting out of the lease.

Beat.

CLEA. Did we?

NEIL. Shouldn't really have access to our number.

Anyway, she sounded . . . odd, kind of . . . hounded –

CLEA. . . . *Hounded*?

NEIL. – Said she hadn't told her flatmate yet, told him she was planning on moving out. Wanted to know if I could talk to the agency on her behalf, speed things up.

CLEA. Well, that's . . .

NEIL. . . . Inappropriate. And then suddenly, she's thanking me, ever so politely . . . and then she's put the phone down. No number or anything. Odd.

CLEA (*half-listening*). Yes, that is odd.

NEIL. I wasn't sure what to say to her.

He puts a pan on the stove, lights the gas and pours oil into it.

Might have to go out again later.

Beat.

CLEA. What, tonight?

She turns and looks at him.

In this?

Beat.

NEIL. Well, I'd like to catch it, out there, while it's . . . it's still . . . I'd like to catch it before it's . . .

CLEA. Make sure you wrap up warm.

She looks back out the window.

And take your camera, this time.

Beat.

NEIL. I will.

Beat.

So, how do you want it?

She looks back at him.

How do you want yours done?

She looks at him, but gives no answer.

You just relax.

She turns back to look out the window.

Better tell Nathan to make good use of me for the next few weeks. Because after that, we are out of here.

Beat.

CLEA. *Gone.*

Beat.

NEIL. I love that smell.

Beat.

Oil, heating up, getting hot.

He throws the steaks into the pan, with a loud sizzle.

She lights another cigarette.

Seems like ages since we've had a holiday.

CLEA *stares out the window.*

NEIL *continues cooking. The steaks continue to sizzle in the pan.*

The lights fade.

Scene Eleven

February, one month earlier than Scene Nine, same month as Scene Four.

SCOTT *and* MICHELLE *are sitting in his flat on the couch, as they finish their dinner, on the coffee table in front.*

Sting plays softly in the background.

SCOTT. I preferred The Police myself. They were good, back then, a proper band.

Beat.

But he's alright for in the background and stuff, you know, in the van.

MICHELLE. Good-looking too, used to be.

SCOTT. Right prat though. He is, he's a right prat.

Beat.

We could put the TV on, if you'd like.

MICHELLE. No. No, this is fine.

SCOTT. Sorry . . . it was a bit overcooked.

MICHELLE. It was fine . . . / nice.

SCOTT. / No, it wasn't. Should of got a pizza. Do ya like pizza?

MICHELLE. Pizza's alright, yeah.

SCOTT. What kind? What's your favourite kind?

Beat.

I like Hawaiian. Though I don't think Hawaiian's eat much ham. Not with pineapple anyway.

MICHELLE. Having someone else cooking, for you. It's . . . nice.

Beat.

SCOTT. Wasn't sure if you'd ring.

Beat.

You sure you don't want the TV on?

MICHELLE. Sure.

Beat.

Nice and warm in here.

Beat.

You lived here long?

SCOTT. No. But I got plans for the place.

MICHELLE. It's big.

SCOTT. Yeah.

MICHELLE. It just needs some little things . . . like lights. You can do great things with light . . . and pictures. You just need to put some pictures up around the place, fill the, the walls.

SCOTT. That's what I thought, yeah. Bought these picture frames, really nice ones, proper glass and that. Nothing to put in them though.

She laughs.

What?

Beat.

MICHELLE. I've got the pictures, photos and stuff, of all kinds of things. No frames. I'm never sure how they're supposed to . . . go up . . . to *stay* up.

He pours them some more wine.

SCOTT. What is that, that . . . smell . . . in your . . . hair?

MICHELLE. Shampoo, probably.

And I use a conditioner, sometimes I use a conditioner.

SCOTT. God, it's nice.

Beat.

It's alright, isn't it? Having a guest? Not as hard as you think.

He gets up, suddenly.

And I, I got pudding.

He goes to the fridge.

Didn't know if you were a cake or fruit girl, like proper pudding, or just . . . like ice cream, or something. Wasn't sure.

She smiles, amused.

MICHELLE. I like all of them.

SCOTT. Well, that's good, because I got one of each.

Beat.

We can do it in stages, start with one and then work through.

MICHELLE. Sounds good.

SCOTT. It's just tinned fruit. What with what's going on out there at the moment, shops seem sort of disorganised.

Like they haven't really worked out what it is that people want yet.

MICHELLE. Yeah.

SCOTT. It's the little things, isn't it? That's what's been . . . affected.

You can only really notice it, if you add up the little things, all at once.

Rest of it just seems to have carried on.

Blink and you'd . . . you'd miss it.

SCOTT *begins opening the fruit, with an old-style can opener.*

MICHELLE. There was this, this scare, on the train, on the way here . . . some bag left at a platform. Happens at least twice a day now, they said, sometimes more.

SCOTT. Shit.

MICHELLE. But turns out it was just some old lady's. They called Security, stopped the trains, made this announcement. And everybody had to wait. And everyone was just so . . .

SCOTT. What?

MICHELLE. I don't know.

SCOTT. Frightened?

MICHELLE. Pissed off.

SCOTT. Were you frightened?

MICHELLE. Of what?

She grins.

Anyway, when they opened up the thing, the bag, it was full of knitting. Little booties and stuff, pink . . . baby blue. Poor old lady, gets off the train and there's all these security guys, waiting for her. Big blokes. Could have given her / a heart attack.

SCOTT *nicks himself with the can opener.*

SCOTT. / Fuck!

MICHELLE *turns round.*

Fuck . . . thing's got teeth. Went right through to the bone.

MICHELLE *gets up, goes to him.*

MICHELLE. Let me have a look.

SCOTT. Shit.

She takes his hands, softly. He seems reticent, tries to pull away.

It hurts. It . . .

MICHELLE. Let me have a / look.

SCOTT. / *Fucking* hurts.

MICHELLE. Let me.

He resists slightly.

SCOTT. You'll get . . . get . . . on your . . . your dress.

She takes the hand again, this time he lets her.

MICHELLE. You got to hold it up.

SCOTT. How can you stand to look at it?

He is watching her closely.

MICHELLE. Just need to apply some pressure, to slow the bleeding.

Beat.

SCOTT. See. I don't know stuff like that. Never did.

MICHELLE. Just common sense. That's all.

Beat.

We should wrap something around it.

Without taking his hand away, SCOTT *leans over and grabs a tea towel.* MICHELLE *isn't happy with his choice of bandage.*

SCOTT. It's alright. I got ten of the things. Bought 'em on special. I'll never use all ten, not for a while anyway.

She laughs.

MICHELLE. You're an idiot.

He looks hurt.

Give it here then.

She begins to wrap the tea towel around his hand, carefully. Eventually he smiles. She is still holding his hand.

See, most people, most people would buy flowers . . . chocolates maybe, but tea towels . . . tea towels. That's different.

SCOTT. They're good tea towels, mind. Proper designs and stuff.

Beat.

MICHELLE. You'll live.

She lets go of his hand.

SCOTT. Yeah, not sure if it's . . . the pressure . . . I think it's still . . .

She smiles, takes his hand in hers again, holds it up. He smiles.

What's it like then . . . your job? Working with kids and that?

MICHELLE. Yeah, I like it.

SCOTT. Part-time, you said?

MICHELLE. Supposed to be. Though I pretty much end up doing full-time, most weeks at the moment.

SCOTT. How come?

MICHELLE. Well, they want people around, all the time, these days. Mums and dads want a familiar face there, every day. Someone they know they can rely on, trust, to leave their children with.

SCOTT. Shouldn't let them do that. Take advantage of you.

MICHELLE. No, I don't, I wouldn't do it if I didn't –

SCOTT. People will do that.

MICHELLE. I like the work, the kids. I like . . . keeping them safe.

Beat.

SCOTT. Well then, that's good. That's . . . good.

MICHELLE. What about you?

Beat.

I mean, do you like kids?

SCOTT. Yeah. Some. The . . . good ones.

Beat.

And the naughty ones. I like them too. Yeah, I like them.

MICHELLE. And I bet the naughty ones like you as well. I bet they . . .

SCOTT. Would you help me?

MICHELLE *looks at him, unsure what he means.*

With the place, I mean. Just help me . . . pick out some lights and stuff, maybe . . . some pictures. Nothing much, just, you know, point me in the right direction. That's all I –

MICHELLE. Yeah . . . I'd, I'd like that.

SCOTT. I could maybe get you some frames.

She lets his hand fall from hers.

Show you how to put them up.

MICHELLE. You don't have to –

SCOTT. I'd like to.

Beat.

MICHELLE. Okay. Yeah, that'd be nice.

Beat.

Where's this pudding you promised me then? I'm ready for the first stage.

SCOTT. You make me want to sing.

MICHELLE (*laughing*). . . . What?

SCOTT. You're *fantastic*.

She smiles.

And every time you do that, that . . . smile, you just keep getting better.

She smiles, looks down at the floor and then back up at him, in the eyes.

MICHELLE. Do you want me to stay? I could.

A pause, it seems as if they are about to kiss, but they don't.

SCOTT. Dunno. First date and everything.

MICHELLE. I don't have to.

SCOTT. I want you to.

Beat.

MICHELLE. You'll have to lend me a toothbrush. Didn't bring anything, didn't want to assume.

Beat.

And it's our second date.

She pats his bandaged hand.

You've been a very brave boy.

She kisses him, quickly, mouth closed, on his mouth.

There. All better.

He looks at her for a moment. Then he takes the back of her head and brings it towards his. He kisses her more firmly.

The kiss is quite passionate, but tender. She responds.

Eventually they break away. A moment.

SCOTT. I knew you'd taste like that.

Beat.

Like . . . like kissing someone, on holiday.

The lights fade.

Scene Twelve

January, one month later than Scene Ten, same month as Scene One.

NEIL *enters, with his camera bag. The lights are off.*

CLEA *is standing at the window, as if looking out.*

NEIL *doesn't see her. He goes to the kitchen and turns the bench light on. He places the bag on the bench and goes to the sink and pours himself a large glass of water, which he drinks. He then refills the glass.*

CLEA. You're a liar.

NEIL *jumps slightly.*

You're a *fucking* liar.

Beat.

You said we couldn't leave until tonight, because of work you said.

But I wasn't sure if we needed to take bedding down, I wanted to check with you before I packed the car.

Beat.

So I tried you at the office.

NEIL *looks up at her.*

They said you weren't there, that you'd left –

NEIL. Clea.

CLEA. – that you'd left the place almost a month ago.

I told them that I'd just rung the number out of habit.

CLEA *looks through the chink in the blind.*

Then I rang Nathan, at the warehouse.

Beat.

NEIL. Clea, I'm . . .

CLEA. And Nathan SAID, HE SAID no . . . he hadn't seen you, that you hadn't helped out down there for the past six months.

I didn't make excuses to him. I just put the phone down.

What have you been doing?

NEIL. You've been / drinking.

CLEA. / I feel dirty. Like I've been . . . I feel dirty, *stupid.*

She moves away from the window, picks up his camera bag.

It's empty.

Beat.

It's fucking empty.

She throws the empty bag at him.

What have you been doing, Neil?

Beat.

WHERE HAVE YOU BEEN?

He can't look her in the eye.

I went through your stuff, turned the bedroom inside out, looking for something . . . *anything.*

NEIL. It / isn't.

CLEA. / I found this.

She holds up a piece of paper.

Names. A list of . . . names. Men, and women. Dates, but no numbers.

You can't be fucking all of them.

Beat.

NEIL. They're just . . . just people.

Beat.

CLEA. People that died?

NEIL. Yes.

Beat.

CLEA. You've been . . . lying to me . . . *lying* . . . for a load of fucking dead people.

NEIL. They were important. They *are* / important.

CLEA. / They're dead!

NEIL. Yes.

CLEA. They are *dead*!

Please . . . Neil . . .

Beat.

I'm frightened. You're frightening me.

Beat.

Tell me what you've been doing out there.

Please.

Beat.

NEIL. I walk.

He looks away.

I just . . . walk.

CLEA. But where to?

NEIL. It doesn't matter.

Beat.

Out there, I just . . .

CLEA. It's more about leaving somewhere. About being somewhere else.

NEIL. Out there . . . I'm needed.

Beat.

CLEA. By who?

Beat.

By who, Neil? You're not making any sense.

NEIL. Sometimes they don't want to be helped.

Because they're still frightened, they're confused.

I can understand that.

CLEA. What do you . . .

NEIL. I went . . . went back to our old flat, our old neck of the woods.

Seems quiet round there.

CLEA. Neil . . .

NEIL. But wherever you are, wherever, you, go, there's always someone now, who needs something.

Someone, in pain.

You can hear that after a while.

Beat.

And sometimes we find each other.

We comfort each other.

We grieve, for / whatever it is that we've . . . lost.

CLEA. / And what are *you* grieving for?

Beat.

What have you lost that you didn't give away?

Beat.

NEIL. And then we go home.

CLEA. Come home.

Beat.

And do these other people, have . . . wives, partners, that they go home to?

NEIL. I don't know.

Beat.

I don't know.

Beat.

CLEA. I've been seeing somebody.

Beat.

NEIL. Yeah. Yes I thought that you might have / been.

CLEA. / A doctor, Neil, a therapist.

He looks up.

He says that I'm suffering. He said that.

Beat.

NEIL. From what?

CLEA. Just . . . suffering.

Beat.

NEIL. Well, in truth we all are.

CLEA. No, but I am, *I am*, Neil. And he's a professional, so he should / know.

NEIL. / This isn't about you.

CLEA. Isn't it?

NEIL. It's about what's happening.

CLEA. What *happened*.

NEIL. What's happening to all / of us.

CLEA. / *Happened*, Neil. *Happened,* past tense.

NEIL. And now we have to take some responsibility.

Beat.

What's happening, what is happening out there now . . . it's been brewing for a while. But now, now it's as if somebody's flipped a switch, and it's on, it's really on, you can feel it. Feel it in the air. It's on. And any moment . . .

CLEA. What was I supposed to do?

NEIL. Any moment now . . .

CLEA. Tell me what I should have done.

NEIL. Because it's there, it's still there, in the periphery . . . still . . . waiting to . . . but we've missed it. I've . . . missed it.

And it's still falling.

Beat.

CLEA. It's over, Neil.

NEIL. Bang.

CLEA. It's over.

Beat.

NEIL. We have to be prepared. We have to make amends.

Beat.

We can't go back now. We have to change.

Beat.

Because otherwise we're lost.

CLEA. We're not, Neil. We're not . . . / lost.

NEIL. / The world's angry, Clea. It has every right to be. It's angry. I can feel that.

CLEA. Neil, you're frightening me.

NEIL. We're all frightened.

CLEA. Why are you doing this?

Beat.

You know, you look like *shit*.

Whatever it is you're . . . doing, trying to . . . it isn't working.

NEIL. We're all frightened, Clea.

CLEA. Not for anyone.

NEIL. We should be.

Beat.

CLEA. Please, Neil . . . stop it.

Beat.

Let me . . .

Beat.

Let me in.

NEIL. I can't.

CLEA. Neil . . .

NEIL. I can't get through to you any more.

CLEA. Get through what!

Beat.

Get through *what*?

You act as if I killed those fucking people myself!

NEIL. That.

I don't know how to get through that.

Beat.

People are *suffering*, Clea, out there, they are *suffering*.

Long beat.

CLEA. And what the fuck do you expect me to do about it?

Beat.

NEIL. I don't expect you to do anything.

He goes to turn away from her.

She grabs him by the arm, takes his hand.

She puts his hand on her face.

CLEA. We came home. We both . . . made it home.

Beat.

It's alright. We can get on with our lives now. Move on.
We're safe.

He tries to take his hand away.

We're safe.

Beat.

Look at me, Neil.

He is trying to turn away, but she holds on.

NEIL. / No.

CLEA. / Please.

NEIL. No, no I don't . . .

CLEA. Look at me.

NEIL. You're . . .

CLEA. It's alright.

NEIL. You're . . . cold. You're / so . . . cold.

CLEA. / I'm alive.

He looks at her.

I'm *alive*, Neil.

Beat.

NEIL (*hateful*). But for what?

Suddenly he is gripping onto her face, hard, as if trying to crush it.

He doesn't let go.

CLEA. You're hurting me.

He is physically riled. He doesn't let go.

You're . . . *hurting me.*

He doesn't let go.

There is the sound of a siren outside, in the distance.

NEIL*'s eyes, head, dart towards the window and* CLEA *uses the opportunity to escape his grip.*

She exits to the bedroom.

NEIL *watches the space that she's made and then turns back to peer out the window.*

NEIL. I wanted to protect you.

She comes back out, carrying a travel bag.

But you don't need me to.

Beat.

And I can't.

She stares at him for a moment.

I can't.

CLEA. They've gone, the tenants. Both of them cleared out.

Beat.

She must have been trying to warn you, when she called.

She carries her bag to the front door, where she stops.

Beat.

I saw the sky.

Smoke, where the clouds had been, just a . . . moment before. The same colour, but moving upwards, instead of side to side, like they're supposed to.

And everything, everything was white and sharp, for that moment.

And it started to snow.

Then you just know, don't you? You know that something's happened. That it's changed. Even though you're still breathing.

Beat.

I thought of you in that moment, your face.

And then you get out.

He looks at her, as if about to speak. He says nothing.

She opens the front door.

Happy birthday, Neil.

She leaves, closing the door behind her.

NEIL *stares at the door for a while. Then he walks to the blinds and looks out.*

He then comes back to the kitchen bench and turns the light off.

He sits down in front of the TV and turns it on, but leaves the sound down.

He picks up a cigarette and then puts it back in its case.

He stares at the screen, which glows for a moment.

Lights fade on him, as . . .

Scene Thirteen

January, one month earlier than Scene Eleven, same as Scene Two.

Lights fade up on the corner of the stage.

There is an empty space, except for a couple of bar stools and a small bar. The feeling of a place that is eternally empty.

A suspended pub TV hangs from the ceiling, playing sport, but with the sound down low.

MICHELLE *sits alone at one of the bar stools, with a large glass of white wine, nearly finished.*

She looks to the TV, half-watching and then back at her drink.

There is something sad about the way she sits.

Eventually SCOTT *approaches the bar. He stands beside her for a while, not speaking, waiting for service.*

Eventually he turns to her.

Beat.

SCOTT. Who's winning?

   MICHELLE *looks up at him,* SCOTT *motions to the TV screen.*

MICHELLE. I . . . I wasn't really watching.

   Beat.

   . . . Them.

I think.

She looks up to the TV screen.

He joins her looking, stands a little closer to her.

SCOTT. Hard to tell sometimes.

She smiles at him. He grins back.

Lunch break?

She looks unsure.

Or you doing a bunk?

Beat.

Make sense to on a day like this. You see those clouds? Gonna snow.

Best to take cover.

He grins.

MICHELLE. I'm . . . I'm waiting for someone.

Beat.

SCOTT. Oh.

SCOTT *shifts, suddenly uncomfortable. Looks around the place.*

MICHELLE. I don't think they're coming.

Beat.

They're not.

I've been here almost an hour.

SCOTT. Probably took you that long to get served.

SCOTT *resumes his close position, leans against the bar.*

She smiles. He looks towards the bar, looks for a barman. Then turns back to her.

MICHELLE. It'll have worn off by now.

SCOTT. Sorry?

MICHELLE. My lipstick. I . . . it's gone, hasn't it?

He looks at her more closely, unsure what to look for.

SCOTT. Na. Na, I think you've still got a bit on.

Beat.

Yeah. A bit.

She nods and then looks up at the game and then back at her drink.

I been delivering stuff, but the traffic's bloody . . . you know. And I fancied a beer and I thought . . . bugger it, you know? That's the beauty of being your own boss. Never been in here before. You?

MICHELLE. No.

SCOTT. Not a bad place. Quiet.

MICHELLE. Yeah.

SCOTT. Bloke'd have to be a right tosser to stand you up though, wouldn't he?

MICHELLE *smiles but looks coyly at her drink, shifts in her stool.*

It's true. He'd have to be. You've got a fantastic smile.

She looks up at him.

Beat.

MICHELLE. Yeah, well, maybe he is a right tosser.

They look at each other for a moment.

SCOTT. Well, I'll drink to that.

Well, I would . . . if I could get a bloody drink.

Beat.

Tell you what, I'm gonna . . . gonna check downstairs.

SCOTT *walks round to the other side of the bar so that the bottom part of his body is covered by the bar. He then mimes walking down stairs, mimes steps, making himself shorter, as he goes, until he is out of sight.*

MICHELLE *laughs, sharp and sudden, covers her mouth with a hand.*

He comes back up, the same trick in reverse, expertly executed.

(*Dead straight.*) Na. Nobody down there either.

MICHELLE *laughs, bashful. He smiles at her. He looks back to the bar and then at the stool in front of him.*

Do you mind if I . . .

He motions to the seat beside her.

MICHELLE. No.

Beat.

I don't.

He sits down on the stool beside her.

SCOTT. I'll just have the one more. I've already had the one. You don't want to have more than a few, do ya? Not in the . . . not in the day. Dangerous.

Beat.

Before you know it, it's dark . . . the whole day's sort of . . . swallowed up.

MICHELLE. I've had . . . I've already had two.

SCOTT. Oh, two's alright. You have two, you see, and it puts a kind of . . . blanket over everything.

MICHELLE *laughs.*

What?

MICHELLE. Nothing.

SCOTT. No, what?

MICHELLE. I don't know.

Pause.

I've had three. I've had three glasses, already.

Beat.

SCOTT. I've had two.

MICHELLE. And I'm not going back to work today. That's it, I've made my mind up. I'm putting my foot down.

She downs her drink, in one.

She puts the empty glass on the bar, he is watching her.

SCOTT. It's your teeth, that's what it is, you know. They're perfectly symmetrical.

She closes her mouth, self-conscious.

No, really, most people don't have that, one side's normally different to the other. But with you . . . they're . . . perfect, all in a neat little line.

Beat.

And it probably means something too . . . like you're a good person, or you're gonna come into money or something.

MICHELLE (*laughing*). What?

SCOTT. . . . Or like you're gonna meet the love of your life. Any day now. I'd say.

Beat.

Something like that.

Beat.

I'm a fucking idiot, aren't I?

She smiles at him. And then goes to get up.

He moves with her, mirroring her move and speed, his move is almost nothing, a reflex, but for a moment it's as if he's standing in her way, for a second. But almost nothing.

Sorry.

He backs off slightly, but stays standing.

MICHELLE. What?

SCOTT. Na, I'm . . . Sorry.

He stares at her.

MICHELLE. I was just . . . just going to go the ladies.

Beat.

Must be all that wine, goes straight through me.

He's still standing in front of her.

But . . . I should be . . .

SCOTT. I'm glad he didn't turn up. The other bloke.

Beat.

Just thought I'd tell you that.

Beat.

She picks up her bag from the bar. She smiles, and begins to walk away.

SCOTT *sits down, deflated.*

MICHELLE *suddenly stops and turns to him.*

MICHELLE. You could . . . could get me another drink.

He looks up at her, unsure of which way to jump.

Beat.

SCOTT. Don't even know your name.

MICHELLE. It's . . . it's Michelle.

SCOTT. *Michelle.*

Beat.

. . . Scott.

She smiles.

Well then, Michelle, what you drinking?

Beat.

MICHELLE. I'll have a . . . a . . . I don't know.

SCOTT. *Anything*, anything you want.

MICHELLE. You choose.

Beat.

Go on.

Beat.

Surprise me.

MICHELLE *turns and exits, smiling. He watches her leave and then turns to the bar, and then up to watch the TV screen.*

On the TV screen, we see that the game is interrupted by a flash announcement. A news reporter stands, trying to make a report, but the transmission is fuzzy, almost inaudible and barely visible, as if being constantly interrupted by something bigger.

SCOTT *keeps watching.*

The lights fade, but the light of the TV screen remains, as the transmission comes and goes and SCOTT *half-watches.*

It continues to come and go.

Until finally it cuts out.

Then blackout.